Between a whisper and a roar

J. Nicole Cohen

BookLeaf Publishing

Presentation by *BookLeaf Publishing*

Web: www.bookleafpub.com

E-mail: info@bookleafpub.com

ISBN: 9789357212304

First edition 2023

DEDICATION

This book is dedicated to my husband, my beloved, my best friend and my partner for life. Also, our beagles, current, former, and future.

ACKNOWLEDGEMENT

I never thought I could write a book, and now here I have...I suppose, I want to acknowledge myself, my efforts and my stick-to-itiveness, here in written form. You did a good job.

I also want to acknowledge that various other artists and things in the world have impacted and influenced me.

PREFACE

"I used to call myself a poet and a girl
I haven't been either in many many years and yet I've started this endeavor.
I just want to tell my story…to myself…to my child…to the world
They haven't heard me in a while and I think I have something to say.
Ex-Devoted cult member…Jesus Freak
Ex-Devoted daughter…
Ex-Pushover Friend…
Half-White
Half-Black
Half-Alive at 33 years old
My Jesus Year
Woah…that never occurred to me until now, I think I still thought I was 32
I am recognizing my age
Recognizing my body and mind changes
And recognizing the loss
Do you know how lonely it is to grow up thinking you have a mother only to learn that you did not?"

Fairy Tales

The men in my family are weavers

Pulling threads of fiction from thin air

weaving them with strings of truth

to make the most beautiful tapestries

Emperors New Curtains

Glass Houses…calling stone-made holes

Stained Glass

Calling blood-spattered shards

Art

Washed in the blood

wolves wearing coats of spotless lambs.

Little Girl Little Girl won't you let me in????

Resemblance

The first man I fell in love with was a lot like my father…

Well except he was shorter, chunkier, hairier, and white.

Here's the story:

Picture it, Sunday Morning 9am...I am sitting in the same church pew I have sat in every Sunday morning for 16 years, my mother to my right, my granny lottie to my left.

Something new flashes before my eyes...a new family? A mom, plain with nice long brown hair, a dad, gruff looking, like he's worked hard, but with gentle eyes...and a guy...curly brown hair...blood red button down...wide leg jeans, no tears, rips, or stains but a pocket chain….

Who is this? We sing, shake hands, hear the same joke, head off to Sunday School…

He's in my class...the only new person in this class in 16 years.

His name is matt...he's new, his parents got saved at a FAITH visit and were joining the church.

Fast Forward>>> We're on the church van going to church camp...we've become friends...he's in love with Amber.
Amber is a b**** (she used to be my idol), she's on her period and complaining and taking up more space than normal...he is fawning over her...asking how he can make her see him...I'm thinking the same thing.

Fast Forward>>>>Another church camp...this time I find out he's a poet. I spend the next night...all night writing poems in the dorm room bathroom...my friends are worried. I show the notebook to Matt and he lights up...reads every word and asks if he can write me some...we have bonded.

Both of our dads are on again off again Alchie's...His more violent than mine when drunk...mine significantly more criminal and mean on the reg. We both love Jesus. Are ecstatic to have a "new father", and I am to be his mentor in all things Church Kid.

Fast Forward>>>Summer's over, school has started...he's a grade above me...has friends that are all hard rock(he plays guitar in a metal band and made me a CD...I fell in love with The Exies...I gave him a playlist with Jason Mraz and James Blunt) we pass notes every day...I sit with him in the hallway...We hug once and I give him a pat on the back...says never do that to a man...it is entirely de-masculinizing...I have learned.

I write a poem…"I love you, is it equal, could this be our life's prequel?" asking him out...he accepts...he is my boyfriend.

We hold hands at church 2 days in a row…

Walking to the practice field flute it tow...on cloud 9 reading a note from my boyfriend...artfully folded…

"You are like my sister...this was a mistake…"

Heart Broken, I sob without missing a step...without missing a chit, I march my show perfectly.

I ball all the way home...my heart is shattered…

Fast Forward...3 months later I work up the courage to ask him for our journal of poetry back...and he says I think I threw it away…

Now I see the resemblance.

The second man I fall in love with is exactly like me...and my father.
Both the children of alcoholics...both in love with queer culture and everything from the internet..
Both entirely incapable of being fully functional adult human beings…
I'm a virgin...He makes me a promise...I will find someone for you to sleep with by the end of the year.

I laugh...I have a dream...I write a tumblr post...I hear a knock on my door

"You wanna get drunk and talk about that post you just wrote???I know it's about me."

Woah...too much too fast...we drink...we giggle...we ultimately fuck…

I am in love. He's a poet...He's an artist...He's cute and self deprecating and my first friend that ever saw and liked all of me.

He's looking for a girl.
I'm not a girl. I'm an in between amalgamation...I'm a queerdo...I'm his bro...his boi...could be more if I was just more feminine...but for the first time ever...I'm not interested in changing…
We date...it doesn't work...I save his life several times...we make forever promises...we are soul mates..Meredith and Christina...but he is not my Augustus Waters...more sobbing...more soul searching.

I fell in love again...with someone else...left him in the way he had left me for her...and he couldn't handle it...needed to be my one and only when I was never ever going to be his…

I see the resemblance.

The man I love now...is nothing like my father…

Nothing at all...He's brilliant, and kind, he's giving and adorable and sweeter than a person has a right to be...and now in this relationship...I am my father…

Expecting more than I am putting in, creating distance where none should be...asking for cliff dives and tightrope walks and leaps of faith with no proof that I am capable of being a safety-net.

I see the resemblance…

Mommy

I miss my mom.
Well…not my actual mom but who she was supposed to be?
My husband and I are trying to have a baby
Something I never wanted but so badly want now
The refrain "A Girl Needs Her Mother" echoes in my head
I'm not a girl…but I needed a mother
How will I be one without her?
How will I be without her?
Who will I be without her?
I guess whoever I am.
Maybe who I've always been?

Send Me Flowers

He requests that I send him his flowers while he is still alive, as if me sending flowers upon hearing of his death is a foregone conclusion. Since being married, my husband and I get a chuckle out of contemplating sending him the arrangement they put around the necks of horses when they win a race, or an artfully composed funeral board arrangement of faux-flowers spelling out "probably got them in just under the wire".

My father has tried for decades to kill himself, isn't that what a crack addiction is?

The man requests flowers as if he expects me to mourn not only his loss but my own, as if I have ever worn anything other than sackcloth and ashes in his presence, as if I am not already haunted by his ghosts…This man demands flowers, but I have plucked the petals already playing doomed games of He loves me He loves me not always ending with bare stems and further proof of the already obvious….

Should I send him dead stems and bruised petals, say I grew these just for you but despite my best efforts I just couldn't keep them alive for the decades I have been waiting for you to

drop off that Razor scooter you promised to send me for my 9th birthday.
I read an honest obituary once, written by an abused child for his abusive father. It said "The Joy this man missed out on is his loss, I owe him nothing, and I have only lost the heft of his weight on my back."
If you request anything less from me than honesty, then you will be sorely disappointed. I am no longer a bless your heart southern baptist, I will not smile at you anymore, bend to you will as the dutiful daughter I used to be.
Jewish folks don't send flowers at death, to avoid the morbid situation of asking someone who is grieving to watch yet another beautiful thing die in their presence.
Maybe upon your death, I'll buy myself flowers, a way to mark a less than literal loss with a metaphor…as the petals droop and the stems weaken…
At least me and my father flowers will get to experience a life cycle together, I'll buy new blooms, see their best days, share my stories, my joys, the mundane aspects of my day, and I will admire his beauty, his bravery in the face of impending death, and I will mourn his loss when that day comes, and I will move on with a beautiful memory, as any child should be able to…

Send me my flowers while I am still alive, He says…
Parent me while I'm still a child…Love me while I still believe I may be worth it….Get to know me while you still have a chance…
By the way dad, I've never gotten any flowers from you.

Foreshadowing

Why did my mommy steal my money the little
boy with the red mouth says matter of factly
This question is rhetorical
He already knows the answer
That is just what mommies do.
Wise beyond his 5 years
He stoops and picks up
what she left behind
pennys, nickels, the occasional quarter
Knowing
even then

he will never have enough.

He taught me mischief #1

The headline read vigilante justice
When you, early 70's, oil slicked grey hair, frankenstein head, sausage fingers and your early 50's Puerto Rican disabled army vet best friend chased down the man who stole your car…after of course, purchasing a replica 2003 Lincoln Town Car to do so.
Best Buddy Cop Movie Ever!
Cornered in the walmart parking lot, the man stops the car and attempts to continue the chase on foot,
You fire a warning shot into the air, surrounded by unsuspecting shop country shop goers
Citizens arrest
The police arrive ask if you want to press charges
You say no, you only wanted your car…and an adventure.

He taught me mischief #2

My Paw-Paw was 5 ft 18 inches
Was sausage fingers, square head, all muscle and work-strengthened back
Was I'll get it done spring o' the year
Was there's a snake in the glove compartment, never open it without me
Was why buy a week's worth when there is a year's worth on the shelves I could buy instead
Was retired air force and runner up for county sheriff
Was iridescent tubs of motor oil dotting the driveway
Was a 4-wheeler without breaks, a go-cart with no seatbelt, a pickup truck with no footwell
Was lifegard and savior when I floated past the pier
Was racist until my sister and I came along
Was I will physically put down anyone who tries to harm my granddaughters including their father
Was sorry we can't go to the ocean this year, someone accidently pulled the plug and we have to wait for it to refill
Was kerosene and gritty orange soap
Was hard work never hurt anyone

Was This ain't the holiday inn
Was a jungle gym
Was a bird whisperer and a sugar free candy inhaler
Was stolen hospital pillow cases because Jughead likes the way they feel
Was go on your trip, I'll be here when you get back, I promise
Was frail and small and still the biggest presence in the room
Was my first vision of a beautiful death
Was a hand reaching out to hold that of his wife and that of his mother surrounded by his family as they sang him out of this world
Was so very here, so indelibly human, so much
Was my model for what manhood and fatherhood could be.

Matthew 7:21-23;25-30

Depart from me I never knew you
Words that struck terror into my young heart
Words I hoped, prayed I'd never hear from the savior I dedicated my life to at the ripe old age of 7. Hell is being apart from Christ.
Not everyone who says to me Lord, Lord shall enter the kingdom of heaven.
Even then I understood that that meant that despite what the preacher said I could not know that I know that I know, so every night I said the sinner's prayer and rededicated my heart, hoping to never be caught unprotected by the blood.
How devastating then to be cast into outer darkness by the blood that runs through my very veins…
Mommy, Mommy, there is weeping and gnashing of teeth.

Jesus Paid It All!

Jesus paid it all
All to him I owe
Sin had left a crimson stain
He washed it white as snow
Except how do I know if I'm actually clean?
I mean do you know, that you know, that you know?
You can't be plucked from the hand of g-d…
Unless you were never actually there in the first place?
I got saved for the first time at 7 years young
After watching a clown mime the murder of his only son in the gears of a drawbridge
And I thought…wouldn't it be nice to have a father like that?
To be sacrificed for instead of sacrificed by…
The problem being that I already did.
The drawbridge operator didn't save his son, didn't prioritize his child, didn't sacrifice himself
I was never going to be his first priority, starting life as a stranger he loved more than his own blood only to be transformed into another child to sacrifice…

Transforming The Word

Jesus…Jeez us…Geez, Us
The Sweetest name I know
We fill my every longing and keep me singing as I go

Geez, us is the rock and it rolls my blues away
bop shoo bop shoo bop woo!

Geez, it's us…without us how lost I would be

Geez us, geez us, how I trust us
How We've proved us o'er and o'er
Geez us, Geez us precious Geez us
Oh for grace to trust us more.

Blessed Assurance Geez Us is mine!

I always found christian love songs to jesus kinda creepy…just like Roommate's interpretation of Rob Bell's Sex G-d (Heaven is eternity spent literally fucking jesus)
but sung as an acknowledgement of the mysterious, magical, transformational love between my husband and I…it's kind of sweet!

Now, when I sing a capitalized He, I am talking about a living breathing mortal man, my Beshua, my beloved, my lower-case savior, my best friend. J.A.C

bell hooks

WHEN I FIRST LEARNED THAT bell hooks
DIDN'T CAPITALIZE HER NAME
I THOUGHT woah THAT COULD BE ME
I COULD RADICALLY,
IRONICALLY,INTENTIONALLY MAKE MY
NAME SMALL
STAND UP FOR THE 4th GRADE KID WHO
TOLD THEIR READING TEACHER THEY
DIDN'T BELIEVE IN CAPITAL LETTERS
AND DIDN'T CAPITALIZE ANYTHING FOR
THE ENTIRE YEAR

I USED TO TRY AND SHRINK MYSELF
DOWN AND NOW THAT i AM READY TO
TAKE UP SPACE
PERHAPS MY NAME, WHERE i HAVE
ALWAYS STOOD UP SHOULD TAKE A
STEP BACK
I HAVE ALWAYS MADE SURE THAT THEY
CALLED ME nicole
WELL MOSTLY
MY FRIEND CALLED ME nickles
MY CHURCH CALLED ME ralph
MY FAMILY CALLED ME nic
MY DAD CALLED ME blackie

I wonder

I wonder what she says when people ask her about me
I wonder if people ask her about me
My sister was the prodigal son
So who does that make me?
I am not the dutiful but angry brother who stayed
Not anymore
I was tired of watching her slaughter my fatted calves because my sister deigned to stop by and visit her children
I was tired of the all-day parties that were thrown in her honor when she returned from what I now know was a bender
I suppose they expected me to sew my wild oats and come back home
Cry forgiveness for dragging their names through the mud
Give them the honor of being the bigger person
I guess now, I'm an unnamed character
There to move the plot along in the beginning
But no longer vital to the rest of the story
I wonder what she says when people ask her about me
Oh, Nicole's fine…(she) always was.

Sex Education

Sex is weird, right?

Not the piece A into Slot B thing we hear in school

Not the Magical blurry visual we get from television

Not the cure or the disease…Everything…Nothing

My single mother never uttered the word sex to me or anything on the subject

But once, I did read the word masturbate in her search history…

My absent father, at the age of 5 or 6, had me draw diagrams of ovaries and testes...label the fallopian tubes…the vas deferens

Said "no man will teach my kids about sex but me"

I remember the slow trace of my pencil over his drawing…

The bumping along the dips and divots of that concrete table in the prison yard…

Like a tongue outlining an areola…

I remember the frustration of not being able to maintain a straight line and not being able to erase the evidence of my mistakes…

Trying anyway only to leave smudges and holes marring the otherwise perfect paper…

Feeling singularly ill-equipped to do the job well

Look what you made me do daddy

My Fear

My worst fear is being forgotten
Not in a leave a legacy type of way
In a Home Alone, Kevin never got on the plane
type of way

That got dark fast…

As a kid, I would pretend to forget first and
avoid this fate
My Kindergarten teacher would wave in the
halls, just one year after being in her class, I'd
walk on blank faced.
My first grade teacher ran into me at a Crawdads
game. I'd make 'stranger danger' eyes and hide,
silent behind my mother.

"Nicole is shy…Nicole, You're being rude"
No mommy, this is self-protection

I ask for our book of poetry back, he says "I
think I lost it…meh"
I ask if he remembers our reading wars and
soccer talent show performance, he says "To be
honest, I've done a lot of drugs since then and
don't remember you at all."

I say "Rachel, how have you been since marching band, it's been what, 2 years?"She points to herself, mouths are you talking to me, shrugs and continues walking down the freezer aisle…

When Karen and Jack sing Unforgettable, I weep every time. This is all I have ever wanted. To know I'd be remembered, just as I remember.

When long-lost friends, family, lovers, reconnect in TV, Books, and Movies, I seethe with jealousy and shame.

I spent a year loving and being loved, knowing and being known, celebrating and being celebrated, but I am not sure that I am being remembered just as I am remembering…

I turned 27, 28, 29, 30, 31, 32, 33 and no one called…
I got married, moved across the country, lost a dog, experienced a global pandemic, and no one called…

Will they learn when I've stopped living? Will anybody care to know?…
I hope they just go read all of my poems, and don't bother with my soul.

Make sure my sister knows I love her
Make sure my mother knows the same
Please know I will never forget you, even if you cannot say the same.

Blood

I have conversations with you in my dreams
Real mother daughter shit
Like
How come you haven't called me in 7 years?
Do you know what it is like to feel replaceable
to your mom?
Huh, I guess you might….
That's the problem with your Hallmark
Adoption Story
As real as found family can be, you've gotta
thread the needle carefully to not hit blood.
Is that why we all have different names?
To continue the legacy of illegitimacy?
I think I always felt them more as grandparents
than you did as parents
And ain't that a bitch
The power children have to hurt their parents
But they never let you go
Even after your grand rejection
They just kept showing up
Never stopped reaching out
Never stopped supporting you
Too bad you don't have their blood
Nature over Nurture I guess

When I was a kid, I knew were were all family
because we all snored
Couldn't nobody tell me nothing different to this
very day
The really fucked up thing is that she is still
unconditionally on your side
Even if I was her Precious Angel #1.
Like mother like daughter…?
I hope it skips a generation.

Honestly?

He calls me more than you do.
He who loved me less.
He who said I looked so much like you that I was hard to look at without flying into a murderous rage.
He the thrower of the rock shattering glass into my car seat
He the kidnapper taking me from band class walking behind me so I couldn't run putting my phone battery into his pocket and handing me back the empty shell
He the force-feeder, He the one who made me run through fire
He the one who buried so much fear in my spirit I am still unearthing its tendrils
Yeah…He apologized today for not contacting me in a while…said he'd like to see me.

Can’t Sleep

My husband sleeps beside me
I lay next to him holding my pen
My thoughts won’t let me rest yet
Today can’t yet come to an end
I spent my morning singing Casting Crowns
Complete with spiritual visions from my youth
The gaping chasm between g-d and man
The warning bells of a once misunderstood truth
The distance cannot be bridged by blood
That is where the songs go wrong
Lifting our masks, bearing our truths
Seeing each other as g-d has all along
The queer movie Latter Days has one of my
favorite discussions of g-d
Comparing his panoramic view with our ultra
zoomed in near pointalist lens
Reminding us to stop assuming and keep
moving
Only g-d can see everyone, everything, and how
it all ends
I loved that concept long before I let go of
loving jesus
Casting crowns sings Daddy Here I am
again…Will you take me back tonight
Apologizing for loving the world

G-d how could I have thought that was right?
I can't sleep yet because I am angry
That I let those lies seep so far into my brain
Believed so deeply I and everyone else was
broken
And kept myself a victim to so much
unnecessary pain

Trials and Tribulations of a Mixed Kid

"Maybe some people go for that mixed stuff, but not me"-Older Black Female Co-Worker

I have just explained how it is important to me to represent diversity when I select books for my curriculum, as a black person.

I have just laid claim to an identity in contention.

I sometimes think I should carry around a picture of my father in my left back pocket to prove my blackness, and my mother in my right to prove my whiteness. Here's my dad, He was in Jail for the bulk of my childhood, is an alcoholic and a drug addict, has a mother willing to make the most outrageous excuses for his behavior, smokes black and milds, I know every word of Lift Every Voice and Sing and have spent many, many hours in an AME church dressed all in white for the first Sunday of the month...Here's my mother she used to wish we had a pickup truck so we didn't have to go to the dump as often and could just fill the back up with bags of trash for a once a month trip…my grandfather put all of my sister's dogs down with his own gun…I was raised Southern Baptist…I owned camo Birkenstocks…I have family members with confederate flag tattoos, I almost wrote rebel flag instead…

Angie wouldn't let me sit with her on the bus in 6th grade, she said she could "Smell the nigger on me.", I had never spoken to her before.

My white girl college "friends" told me I was only in the same scholarship program as them because I was black and came from a broken home.

Cayla's dad celebrated his daughter's birthday in his bedroom because she invited that colored kid. He couldn't bear to sing to his daughter at the same time as me.

My flute section friend Amanda called a boy a Mixed Monkey and an Oreo while I was seated beside her…I said "Hello?", and she said you're mostly white so it's ok, I wasn't talking about you.

I have always felt too black to be white and too white to be black. Only in adulthood did I realize that blackness was big enough to hold me and to solely claim whiteness would be a farce. How then did this grown ass woman in 2016 have the audacity to tell me that I was not black to her. To ask me to refrain from claiming my actual identity in her presence, angry that I explained myself in the same words she uses to explain herself.

I nodded respectfully and made it to the restroom just before the hot tears escaped my eyes.

In the 4th grade my school took a trip to a historical all black school house. When the tour guide finished explaining that only black children went to this school and only white children went to the school up the road a kid raised his hand and said "Where would Nicole go?" The tour guide without thinking said To be honest Nicold would've probably been aborted…or at the very least not been able to go to school anywhere, it's not like you can't tell.

Fury and shame battled for dominance leaving me shaking and confused, once again unsure of my footing on a bisected foundation. A foot in two worlds is stability in none.

A survey I took recently allowed me to fill in my own race, this is what I wrote–I am a Bi-Racial Black American with a white mother and a black father, I do not fit inside of a generalized check box system, most forms are not ready for me…Thank you for making room for me to take up space.

My Body

I wanted to love my body before I put a baby in it.
At least know my body,
Here is what I know so far.
I am hairy as fuck, and I don't hate it.
I stopped shaving my legs in high school, I had only started because a bully told me I should in the girls locker room in 6th grade with a look of utter disgust on her face as I propped my shoe on the bench beside her to tie my laces….I didn't know I had more to be ashamed of, I had already squeezed my fat body into the stall to change my clothes for gym…didn't know there was more I needed to do…
I love the feeling of the breeze lifting the hair on my legs, the way my armpit hair wicks sweat away from my skin and my clothes.

For You

I will probably call you daughter or son
At least until you show or tell me different.
More than that, I will call you intentional,
wanted, chosen, planned and prepared for.
You will look at your father and say, I know why
my mom chose you and you will look at me and
say I know why dad chose you.
You will know that you are worth every effort,
every sacrifice, every tear and hopefully know
nothing at all about any of those things until well
into your own adulthood.
You will be laughed with not at
Comforted not asked to comfort.
You will know what it is like to be held,
respected, praised, pushed, appreciated, trusted,
delighted in, listened to.
You will be read to and sung to.
You will be told stories and tickled and kissed
and held and taught to self soothe and made to
feel safe.
These promises I make to you, alongside your
father.
Our most cherished future child, my evidence of
things unseen.

www.ingramcontent.com/pod-product-compliance
Lightning Source LLC
Chambersburg PA
CBHW051743130826
49812CB00033B/986
* 9 7 8 9 3 5 7 2 1 2 3 0 4 *